O .rm

BRYANT-MOLE, Karen

On the farm

First published in Great Britain by Heinemann Library, Halley Court, Jordan Hill, Oxford OX2 8EJ,
a division of Reed Educational & Professional Publishing Ltd.

OXFORD FLORENCE PRAGUE MADRID ATHENS MELBOURNE AUCKLAND KUALA LUMPUR
SINGAPORE TOKYO IBADAN NAIROBI KAMPALA JOHANNESBURG GABORONE
PORTSMOUTH NH (USA) CHICAGO MEXICO CITY SAO PAULO

Designed by Jean Wheeler
Commissioned photography by Zul Mukhida

Printed in Hong Kong / China

01
10 9 8 7 6 5 4 3 2

ISBN 0 431 06319 2

British Library Cataloguing in Publication Data
Bryant-Mole, Karen
On the Farm. - (Images)
1.Farm life - Juvenile literature
2.Farms - Juvenile literature   3.Readers (Primary)
I.Title
630

Some of the more difficult words in this book are
explained in the glossary.

Acknowledgements
The Publishers would like to thank the following for permission to reproduce photographs. Bruce Coleman Ltd; 5 (bottom) Thomas Buchholz,
12 (right) and 13 (right) Hans Reinhard, 13 (left) Harald Lange, 15 (right) Fritz Prenzel, 20 (left) Andy Purcell, Positive Images; 14 (right),
21 (left), Tony Stone Images; 4 (right) and 20 (right) Peter Dean, 5 (top) Raymond Gendreau, 8 (left) Howard Grey, 8 (right) Brian
Atkinson, 9 (right) Kevin Horan, 12 (left) Andrew Sacks, 15 (left) Peter Cade, 21 (right) Zigy Kaluzny, Zefa; 4 (left), 9 (left), 14 (left).

Every effort has been made to contact copyright holders of any material reproduced in this book. Any omissions will be
rectified in subsequent printings if notice is given to the Publisher.

Contents

Fields

Many farms have fields.
There are lots of jobs to be done
in the fields.

ploughing

planting

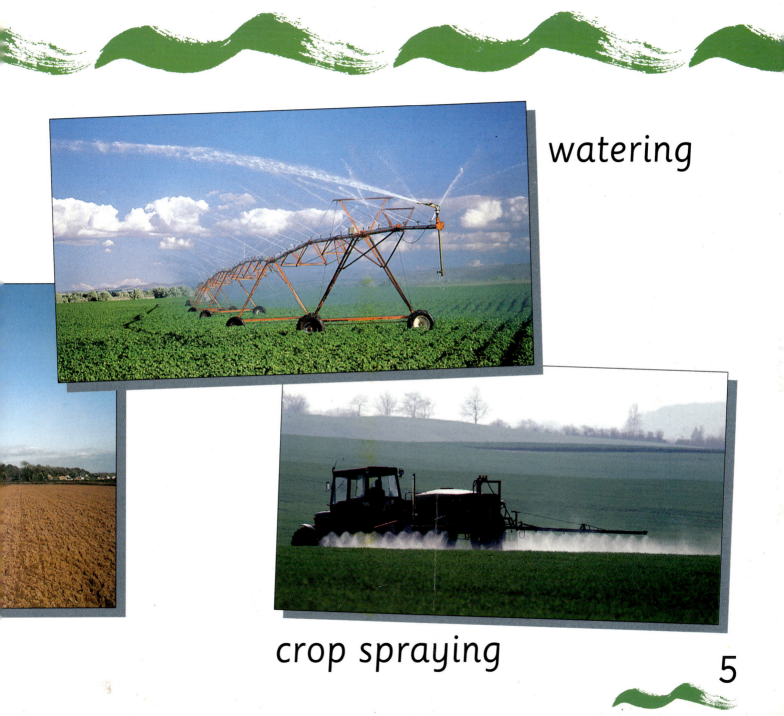

watering

crop spraying

5

Cereals

Some of the crops that farmers grow are plants known as cereals.

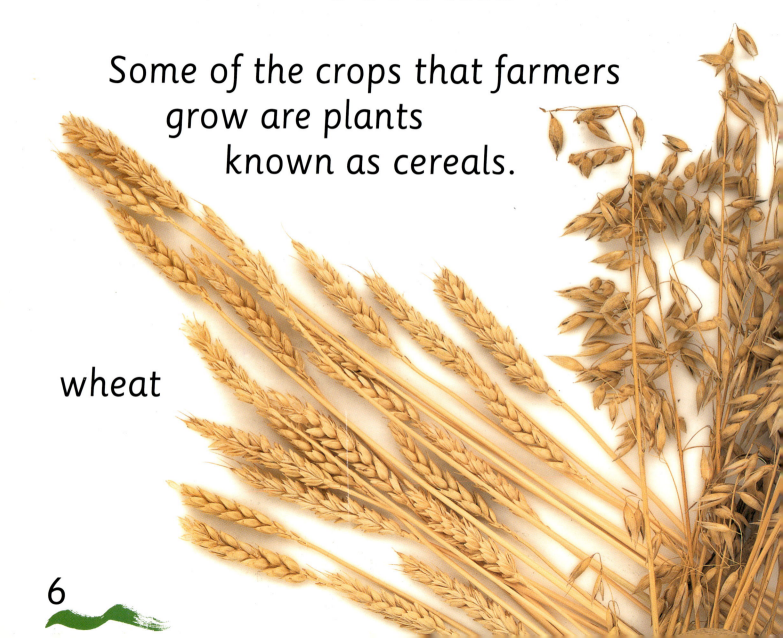

wheat

The plants below are all cereals.

oats

barley

7

Harvest

Cutting or picking the crops is called harvesting.

These crops are being harvested by hand.

These crops
are being
harvested
by machine.

Market gardens

Fruit and vegetables are grown on farms known as market gardens.

11

Animals

Animals are kept on some farms.

turkeys

goats

Have you seen any of these animals on a farm?

geese

hens

Baby animals

Do you know the names of these farm animals and their babies?

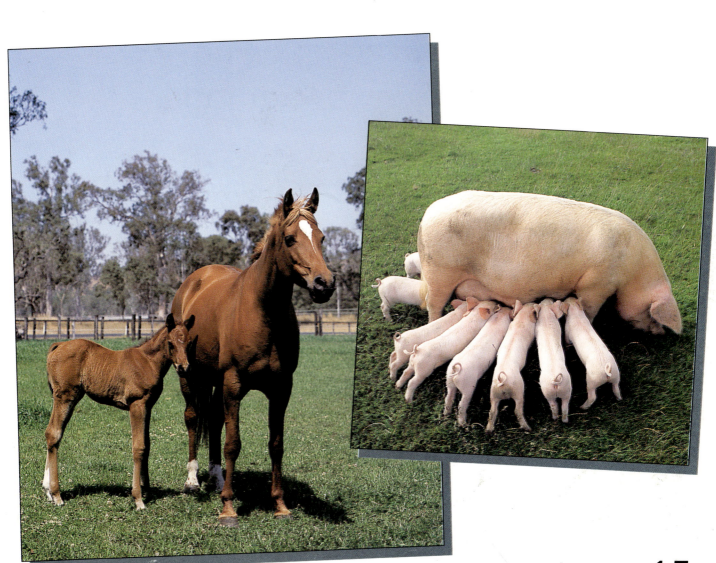

Food

Different animals have their own special food.

hay for horses

corn feed
for chickens

cattle cake
for cows

sheep nuggets
for sheep

17

Clothes

Farmwork can be dirty, noisy and dangerous.

These clothes protect different parts of the farmer's body.

boots

gloves

ear
protectors

19

Machines

Farmers use machines to help them with their work.

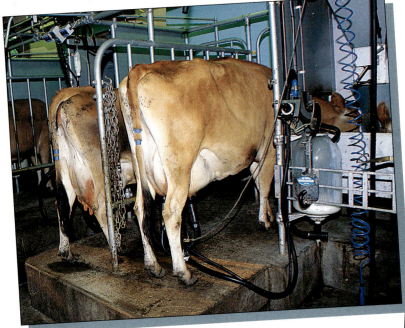

milking machine

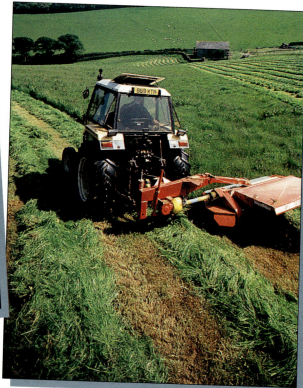

grass cutter

combine
harvester

hedge cutter

21

Collections

If you visit a farm, you could collect some things to remind you of your visit.

Make sure you
ask the farmer first.

Glossary

cereals special grasses with seeds that can be eaten e.g. wheat, maize, barley, rice, oats and rye
combine harvester a machine that cuts cereals and strips off the seeds
crops plants grown on farms
ploughing turning earth over
protect keep safe

Index